I0889324

A Kinder Sea

Felicity Plunkett is a Sydney poet and critic. Her first book, *Vanishing Point* (UQP, 2009), won the Arts Queensland Thomas Shapcott Poetry Prize and was shortlisted for several other awards. She has a chapbook, *Seastrands*, in Vagabond Press's Rare Objects series and is the editor of *Thirty Australian Poets* (UQP, 2011). She has a PhD from the University of Sydney and is a widely published essayist and reviewer. Felicity was the recipient of *Australian Book Review*'s 2019 Patrons' Fellowship.

Felicity **Plunkett**

A Kinder Sea

UQP

First published 2020 by University of Queensland Press
PO Box 6042, St Lucia, Queensland 4067 Australia
Reprinted 2020

uqp.com.au
reception@uqp.com.au

Cover design by Sandy Cull, gogoGingko
Author photograph by Fiona Doherty
Typeset in 11.5/14 pt Bembo Std by Post Pre-press Group, Brisbane
Printed in Australia by McPherson's Printing Group

Australian Government | Australia Council for the Arts

The University of Queensland Press is assisted by the Australian Government through the Australia Council, its arts funding and advisory body.

A catalogue record for this book is available from the National Library of Australia.

ISBN 978 0 7022 6270 8 (pbk)
ISBN 978 0 7022 6384 2 (epdf)

University of Queensland Press uses papers that are natural, renewable and recyclable products made from wood grown in well-managed forests and other controlled sources. The logging and manufacturing processes conform to the environmental regulations of the country of origin.

FSC
www.fsc.org
MIX
Paper from responsible sources
FSC® C001695

For my children

I wish you a kinder sea.

– attributed to Emily Dickinson

Contents

Grace

Heartland

Sound Bridge

My son sings the *Lacrimosa* in Hodonín: joy-
bright teens with a hundred Moravian choristers. Lurch
and tangle, the holding, the letting-

go. Light in his eyes, love. Last part of the last
piece Mozart transcribed, unfinished. We finish
nothing. Others will complete what we have

started: parents, teachers, struck as by felt-covered
hammers while they make notes from loss. Heart-
flange, but no – *No hearts in poems*, says my novelist friend.

Lacrimosa dies illa: all day grief's weft across joy's
warp. Quiet music: tension, strings and frame
of what we can't teach, because we are still

learning: what I can't protect you from, can't
come close to, must damper, love. Words untrans-
latable, but we feel their heft, close: light

as breath. As in the piano's belly, a bridge. The young
composer, eight final mournful soaring bars, echoing
Handel, Bach, solace, the stretch between then

and now. And now, if we are lucky, an angel
strikes us into song. It's the same bridge
to love, for us all: Mozart, Dylan, Rilke – *Who,*

if I cried out, would hear me? The same
question, same notes in new throats, same lesson strung
across centuries, wound strings out of a dark

cave. And angels, when we meet them, might
whistle and have beards, or backpacks and Latin alight
with gain, and again you feel you want to – *can almost* – sing.

A Corner of the Sea

Whether my bark went down at sea –

– Emily Dickinson

Becoming the Sea

after Chris Marks's Imagine Becoming the Sea

I have unreeled sentences from my spine's spool
to free my bones: cast words into the depths

of your response. This morning I gave your name
to the waves, wrote it over mine: palimpsest

proof that will undo me. The sea mutes my words.
They seep, touch nothing, cross straits of black and white.

Last night your laughter across the wake: unimpeachable
love the charge, self-banishment my sentence.

I want you to find me. I want my disappearance to be
untranslatable. Feeding prayers into the sea's throat

I run as fast as ink but we are both dissolving:
when I reach you, we become a corner of the sea.

Glass Letters

A poem […] can be a message in a bottle, sent out in the – not always greatly hopeful – belief that somewhere and sometime it could wash up on land, on heartland perhaps.

– Paul Celan

1.

Your absence sharpens the sea's teeth.
Dear you, days have passed since my last

confession. Words wash
and maul me. How diligently we fish

for a noun to release
our correspondence into grace.

I test the angle of the stars to find
altitude: distance from dissolution, a place

to anchor. When I try to write you
near, my words break the sea's caul, tear

solitude, foam into hymn. Your aria
drowns at the surface of becoming.

2.

If you hear this, my syllables have arrived:
sand-scuttling sidelong.

At sea since you landed, I ask its depths
to vanish the unfathomable.

How small the rest looks, as though a replica
of life: the work of careful crafting.

How much I prepared to meet you:
smoothed myself to sharpen your focus.

Joy leapt into my throat to take breath's
place. Light of head and heart, we seemed to speak.

The miraculous showed me her face: naked
as your arrival would be. No words. No words.

3.

This morning want-of-you has left me.
I test for its absence, press bruises, look clear

in the sea's flat glass. No sign of storms' spines:
sharp possibilities. Disturbance has bled

itself out. Shaken wordless, I wash syllables
in salt, trace remembered promises to

the place they rolled in foam. You
erase waves from our correspondence:

excise agitation. My words stand alone
jittery: banished testimony, punctured. Sutures

loosen in your silence. I rehearse frayed
prayers, word-froth, horizon-bound.

4.

Dark sea-flats, now you are lost to me,
splint against moon's measure, holding

doubt and prayer, reflecting nothing: stasis
where you were. To get used to seeing

alone: to watch a soft-striped sky and not
begin to capture trace and hue.

Is it enough to bottle words, enough
to write and then let go? To lob them

from my craft, discard
the unspeakable, rocks in its pockets?

Hand them to the sea's cur-
ation: a future heartland?

5.

The thought that a skull might be read, its angles
measured like the moon's: bald, resplendent.

Tender shoulderblades that night:
each vertebra precise, ladder-like

as I watched, several rows behind,
saw disappointment curve his back

when he could not see me, sensed the moment
music entered him: imagined fingers

tightening on his arm, felt the world soften. Slap
and shriek of sea-noise now, atonal chords

and wind-song in the rigging. My syllables trace
the gale: Do not follow. Do not forget.

6.

Fierce weather. Soft as shoreline
the terrible declines no chart shows.

Beyond course, maps console no-one.
Where eagles ride the thermals, open water

pours cold against hope. Brine
and absence pickle

your arrival. Forgotten, why force
scrolls into bottlenecks? The plod

of upward blood and down, the mechanics
of onwards   onwards. I can

hardly think. But do. Of you, mainly. Of words
to extract, roll small, send on their way.

7.

Tonight, under the blood moon, I imagine
you here, cresting consolation's wave, cutting

down solitude's hanged man. Shock of warm
breath carrying voice, as when I heard

your secret name. Its small chime and charm
soft on my neck, its kiss, lips edging

my mouth. Cards dealt: fate, pro-
gnosis – beyond small things like

volition. Most nights I find you
on the shore, combing for words

walking shorelines through the liminal
hoard that holds our correspondence.

8.

Name a mouthful of earth, your words bloom
like bread, opening

froth-skirted roses in an old garden
each syllable discarding its petal

under my ribs. Belief in you a root
my hands plunge to pull at: evidence of life

grit under nails, between teeth, silting
organs that once rang clear. Sure, pulsing

your rhythm of heel on soil, of earth pushing
back to affirm you: seeds, yeast and blood

that might go either way. Under me
sea floor: vagrant, shifting, distant.

9.

My flower-filling lungs and kidneys petal-
smooth. Each vertebra

a soloist, fretted: chapters falling a-
way, history unbinding skywards. What I hear

you never spoke. Listen,
they enter, knotted and frayed, our words

a smooth braid in sky's hymnal.
Impossible consolation, songs of wild drift:

flower-scented like an angel's presence,
melodies of exile beaten

permanent by rhythms of human
breath, pressed close in our mutual privacy.

10.

Here the earthed world is gold.
There, waves mean yellow grass blade-edged

thigh-high, fields ablur:
skin spore-prickled and voices rising

like tiny birds, cresting in flight
air currents like gold-flecked fish, up

like ants scaling my leg while waters
ran the other way, hot in child wild

daisy chain and hopscotch play, thump
and jolt of bodies earthing. The swing

lurch and sway, our rush of flight
towards the earth's red throat.

II.

In the distance he is turning on a lamp,
settling into the sofa with a book, thinking

of my body alongside his: thigh by thigh,
limb after limb, waves across softness.

The opening of him to me: promising calm
like a breath-held pause between waves.

Glance into the street that runs
down to shore. His present pours

into night-black silence
still as reprimand, or perhaps

reprieve. I have no words to console, no
way to close the blind, turn down cold's blaze.

12.

I sail away from perjury. You mute your prayer
for life. I wash sky's ceiling with softness. You

study clouds' thesaurus for one close word. I
squint to thread an invisible needle. You

pick at horizons' stitches. I fold desire into hidden
seams. You are gold lining cloudpromise.

I fray the edges of an impossible fabric. You practise
gentleness and knead your faith. I stay away. You

wish me exactly what I wish you, when I
long for nothing: its gold, hearth, yellow. You

are the oblique arm of an angelic generosity. I
am the last sun-glint on a storm-recovering sea.

Anomiidae

Where
the sea has eaten your heart
your edges sharpen, gold. Where
waves' roll
has folded you, bold
small parts
amber the sand. Where
wafer-notes of a lost
shanty jingle underfoot:
exfoliant song-shapes.
Where
sea sieves
a life's pieces and keeps the gleaming. Where
through your lens
the world slips
gold like a fish
a ray
caught in foam nets, shorelines'
curation. Where
your halved bivalve means
solitude, no-one to close
into. Where
translucent hours cut loose
flower gold, each petal aflame.

What the Sea Remembers

Haul and wail of seabirds
who make it mirror and bowl

Rough lines that disclose
its crawl into land, its hold

Discarded stuff, repository
of the wave-tossed, shell-

fracture, plastic, breakage
atlas, axis

trashed and washed. Mossed
plants, laid out to cure

You remember. You chorus
dies irae. White roar

of trauma, of recall. Froth
and spit of weeping. Trace

of all forgetting
Relics of a life, however brief

Vast archive, take my grief's
small file. Cradle

our bodies, undo them, organ
by organ: our sea dead, our lost

to earth. Never buried. Stamp
your name on all you set free.

Trash Vortex

the second angel poured out his vial
upon the sea; and it became
as the blood of a dead man

– Revelation 16:3

In the Great Pacific Garbage Patch, plastic
chokes *Sargassum muticum*, manacles
its ankles, stills its floating liberty, blunts
the blades of laminae: vagrant, strangling.

The Sea of Lost Ships is now a museum
of discards: six kilos for one
of plankton. Seabirds' stomachs
collect bottle tops, balloons: the bright
broken, the dazzling foregone.

Dark ocean, pulse and hope of us:
what have we done? We have sewn
your floor with trip-wires, cut
the cord to our survival.

The sea is dying, gorging on
trash, shame, debris. Then where
to stage the turning-back
of impossible questions
of durable human refusal?

Carmine Horizon

the clouds are shredded along a carmine horizon

– Mireille Juchau, *The World Without Us*

Syzygy

Edge, swerve, disturb, you're all
verb: pressed to you, wilfully
irresistibly, like ivy, sighingly, I climb like
an adverb unattached, insouciant, this high-
wire, thighs and strive, brine and hive, like
glide and tine: riskily, out along the wire
wildly shuffling the letters I have to find
my lines, a sign: my evergreen, my ground-
creeping, my *Hedera rhombea*, my
Araliaceae, my nouns, my verbs, my rising
to scale these outcrops, my um-
bel, my unlobed adult leaves, my
fertile flowering stems, my
marginal list of small words to hold

the edges of other words, fold
into yours like buds or lovers, and my
you are fine, high-scoring, blithe, you
spell out my secret names (bind-
wood, lovestone), syllables
no-one uses except to access this
bingo, palmately, this lucky hand, this
random allocation, all squiffy squeeze, as I sigh
against artery and inferior rib in the crush
of these tiles and us, defying windfall damage, my
greens deepen, words like birds arrive
to disperse seeds like leaves, until my –
like a happy hand of letters, like
za or qi, and quixotry – this syzygy.

Yellow

The stain of love
Is upon the world
– William Carlos Williams

I.

Love-stained day
after day stutters yellow
yellow. Aureate, xanthic,
surprising as a giant canary,
you have flicked a switch, love.

2.

Big. Big as loneliness.
At our wedding he cried
and cried. She darkens, shoves
scrambled egg into a child's mouth.
The joy of having once
been wanted congeals. She spoons
a final mouthful.

3.

Intravenous gold, you
bubble under my skin
like joy, like lust: blister
and hum. Affection and want slop bright
like fat in a surgeon's basin.

4.

Peel back epidermis, dermis: papillary, reticular:
in the *stratum subcutaneum* nerves
roll and spring
like a clock's workings: a
butter-and-honey retirement
token. Love, you are permanent
as the dissolution of duty.

5.

Each egg drops like a lover's
eye, watches then looks away
catches your glow
and throws back a promise
of sleep-fracturing cries.

6.

F. Scott Fitzgerald invented his.
My epigraph is flipped:
west and east eggs easy over
with all this trampolining.

yellow-hatted, yellow-radiant,
high-jumping love:
I must have you!

Songs in a Red Key

Doctor, I have swallowed a glass
alphabet. Syllables sting
and scrabble, *nephro* and *cysto*
herd every shard onside:
compose an edgy mutiny

I need your blade to unstring
me, song's puppet: shaking
humming, undressing, putting on
slash-backed robes of distress
as though for some mortuary
curtain call, where jagged
breathing staggers still
from each of us laid cool
in Ward EM-U 4-2

red keys please

Unlock a tuning fork from its hook
with your secret code. Soothe
chattering toy and tin
carousel wound by pain-keys: slow
them with a quick pry
of morphine's lullaby

Now a broom-choir sweeps
and sweeps panic, blunts
insurgency's sharp bars
clears an angular cacophony
My false notes fall
under the spell
of your attention: my disastrous
overture drops into oblivion

red keys please

Conduct a river in plastic over
my shoulder through an elbow's fold
My shroud stretches to fray
translucent at its seams, rolled
soft by the smooth stones
of a queue of injured
bones: white-gowned, awkward

-ly sheeted nativity
angel, nameless, I shepherd
drip chamber and tremble-wheel
trolley across night's locked ward
jitter this tangle through
silence: my hubris muted
below drugs' sea levels

red keys please

By morning, words have passed
I drift to the light. Outside
the bright miracle flashes
its trashy smile beyond
the signs: *St Vincent's Hospital*
will not tolerate violence
Night's shadows lose their hold
The day fractures in silence

Worn soft in my veins' hive
new feet order their rhythms:
prosody neonate-fragile
dreaming of song and flight, ready
to batter jamb, sash and snapped
cord: open into air

Yellow (On Edge)

Lemon
            pyramids, art ripe
for tumbling
Shiny as Celeste
a scooter named by Una, at three
& favourite
of Anjelica, who sees it
in the centre of many flowers
Soft
            it is lemon
morning walls
before sun turns its back
& my room fades
to the colour of retreat
Harsh
            a skirt I wore
in a pink generation, stubble-
sanding my thighs
smooth as hope
            It is sand, counting
hours towards the day
it will be torched
into glass
Pears
            beyond green
like the melt-and-grain texture
of a dream
before you opened the door
that you would

It is doors
blinking between grey carriages
of people facing forwards
& the colour of illusion:
halo, dream, star
A car, bright
highlighter tracing me
to an apartment
where you won't wait long
Music & indecision push, buttery
at sill & threshold
& break
pierced yolk
running as forewaters as
a hook breaks
the caul
fontanelle-first
it is descent
into arrival
& the coward colour
sharpening my veins
as I arrive
My faith flickers, lighting up
your ruptured patience
& it is tilt, with its small wheels
trembling towards charge

Confetti by Dada

a lie that I have FIXED like a
butterfly on a hat

– Tristan Tzara

Prepare your confession.
Write it out.
Confiteor: I confess.
Now tear your words into flakes:
confetti. Lying,
like any habit,
takes thirty days' abstinence
to break. Create new
neural connections.
When you feel embroidery
or forgery
rising on your tongue,
knit, shell peas,
smoke.

Truth-making as millinery:
embroidery, pinning,
confection. Give me
words close
to what I would choose myself,
if I could afford it.
Not some fine-bone ornament –
the coy-headed shepherdess
of conversation –
fragile, unnecessary
and which I'll have to dust.

Thoughts (venial)
words (bitten
back, or spat
like a nightmare's teeth):
what I have done
and failed to do.
Omission courts commission.
No new messages.
His silence
on any occasion involving
salt, water, prayer
cuts out my tongue.

Cut it out.
Open his love letters.
Take a pair of scissors.
Snip each word.
Place yourself gently
in a bag and shake.
Your portrait emerges
rare, ordinary, interchangeable:
lips, adore, golden, dark, I.

(I still consider myself
very likeable.)

Cyclone Plotting

The danger is that we'll drink this *one quick drink* too fast. The
danger is that one vodka beckons, flirting, to the next. The danger
is that, catching vodka's white wave, I could spill, purple. The danger is
that I will become a nest of matryoshka dolls, falling out of myself. The danger is that
your umbrella, stripping its black veils one by one, will spoke my eye. The
danger is that the rain, hard, will fill the streets with people, pushing. The danger
is that with the smallest shove I'll miss my train. The danger is
that your every gesture, like a Cocteau film, must be deciphered. The danger is that
if I'm not lifted out of this hot storm everything will open, slippery and roof-shaking.
The danger is that I have invented you, and your hip bumping mine promisingly. The
danger is that the rain will wash away my lightning-flash glamour. The danger
is that you feel my softening. The danger is that you know it already. The danger is
that my rained-on hair cannot pretend to be a satin sheet. The danger is that
the only umbrella I have is paper, crimson and stuck in my third drink.
The danger is that I am well out of my depth in this gutterless downpour. The
danger is that you feel the mercury's rise and rise. The danger
is that you don't feel its rise, retaining your leather-jacketed cool. The danger is
that I am making this up out of nothing. The danger is that.

In Search of the Miraculous

Whether she met with gales –

– Emily Dickinson

Equal Footing Mermaids

i.m. Donald Crowhurst born 1932, lost at sea 1969

I. THE LEDGER OF THE DEEP

Her arm raised over
an unbreaking bottle
and the racked smile
of a woman in labour.
You do not preserve love
in the backswing, but in the moving
-forward. She hands you freedom's
echoing hull: loved or revered
fructive, barren, feared.

Too late to call
a thing by its unbroken name.
You sail away
from four children
floating like refugees.
Your boat at the centre
of this marriage
resists all sacraments.

2. HULL

To drift without power or sails
peace that passeth understanding
to remake the world.
There is no god, there is all god, you
are the divine creator of it all.
The shell. An empty place:
ampleness or emptiness of self
that exceeds the hull.

Make a hull: scoop out insides
prow and stern, pelvis and ribs, handfuls
of stuff you are made of:
the smooth and slippery
velutinous and strange.
Bail until self's fabric
billows, frees
itself towards god
and mercy.

3. SHERRY PARTY

Your seasonal telegram:
STRICKEN GOUT FOLLOWING
NEWYEAR SHERRY PARTY
NOW EQUAL FOOTING MERMAIDS STOP
ALMOST INTO FORTIES
At thirty-six no
descent into middleness but this
valorous sloop de loop.
Into the face of BBC camera
and microphone:
'And now let's have something merry!'
God Rest Ye Merry Gentlemen
as it happens: glorious
self-elegy with
drowning harmonica.

4. HORSE LATITUDES

Dolphins fold back
and solitude is a fresh scar.
In the ocean-framed Sargasso Sea
(Mariners' Graveyard and
Sea of Lost Ships)
you will lie forever.
Around you, plants float free:
self-fertile, stretching axils of leafy laminae
towards a vanishing sun.
Sargassum muticum, also
horsetail tangle (inextricable knot)
wireweed (thorncrown for the drowned)
gulfweed (between now and afterwards)
natans (what we are born
into, discover, bequeath).
In the Sea of Expanding Shapes, enter
a vision: fast, meticulous, intense.
The ocean floor ripples. Lost
bones roll towards
your advent,
your disappearance.

Underwater Caulking

after Robin Knox-Johnston

Separated, alone at sea
for the ten lunar months
it takes to make a child,
you discover grief
like someone diving into a dark
envelope of undersea rock
to find a dream's bones.

Penance and confinement,
mending by manual,
the practical magic of canned food
and a stack of classics:
Thackeray, Tolstoy, Melville.
A sea burial for sorrow
far from sympathy
and silence, like an injured animal.
Cabin fever as a cure
for marriage.

Under you the floors
are working loose.
Flake by flake, your craft
comes apart like a pledge.

Leaking bilges
stain the hull:
occluded mourning.
Above, you tend the air
jibs and mizzens,

secure your stays,
listen to Gilbert and Sullivan,
sing along, at night, after
brandy ration and tinned dinner.
The strain may be invisible
but ignored, everything will collapse:
the horse and the rider
are drowned in the sea.

Languid caulk floats out
from secret seams, undoing
compression.
You think of a woman letting
down her hair.

You dive, disguised
from sharks and other devils
in a deep-blue shirt and jeans,
knife strapped to your leg,
impossibly hammering
dry caulk into weeping seams.

The shadow fish traces you.
You haul yourself up,
frangible heart stuttering
loud in your loneliness.
Swift-dealt cards,
faster for the adrenaline:
spare the shark, sink waiting,
shoot the shark, calling others
grey and curious into a mesh of
blood, convulsion, guilt.

This is solitude, then,
eat or be eaten;
the least bad choice
and scraps of possibility
leaking like bloodribbons.
The shark shot, you dive
into dark wounds.

I still worried about the floors,
but no more than I worried
about the keel bolts
or hull fastenings.

Within days, you enter the Doldrums.

Disappearing Act

i.m. Bas Jan Ader born 1942, lost at sea 1975

because gravity overpowers me

– Bas Jan Ader

Things tilt,
                    fall
over and we
do: stasis a moment
before the forwards

        jolt.
        In a slippery-shingled world
gravity became your ludic friend –
your *avant* heavy with visions
of afterwards.

Your early work charts
falls: 'Broken Fall (organic)' from a bike
into an Amsterdam canal; 'Broken
Fall' into a trestle;
from a chair perched
on the roof, becoming
again the bundle your mother
threw to make
an impossible escape. 'Fall I'
(Los Angeles 1970)
can neither forget nor recall
Winschoten 1944.

For you at two
your father's execution
meant only abandonment.
Resistance, courage, harbouring
the persecuted: ideas beyond
the world of your days.
The words of your work collect
a toddler's small syllables
PLEASE DON'T LEAVE ME.

A film so stark
(then a postcard, another
film, a photo)
that unstopped tears
collect all tears:
'I'm too sad to tell you'
testimony of one who saw
but could not phrase –
particles of innocence
particles of witness.

And learning through this
grief's isolation
and the falling of all art –
thoughts unsaid,
then forgotten

At the end
'In Search of the Miraculous' –
a lonely voyage

a-

cross

the Atlantic

to fall into the vanishing point

no roof, windows
tilt, no earth

all

tilt: the sea's windows
opening to the miraculous.

Grave-craft

I. FALL

After they shot your father
the Germans gave
your mother
fifteen minutes

to prepare herself
and her children
for
arrest

gravity

You were standing there

as she flung clothes
out of windows

expression

gravity

Each garment fell: shot bird
or grief disclosed

'All My Clothes'
your flung birds
remember what you saw

In those fifteen minutes
you fell
                out of the present tense

                gravity
abducted you
and your childhood

                                arrested

Craft and grave
grave-crafting
the memory of your graveless father
led to the end by resistance

                gravity

                irresistible

fifteen minutes
crafting gravity:
                                grave-
                                                crafting

2. NIGHTFALL

Trauma is a battered craft
that circles back towards its own arrest.
I am trying to say the same thing, another way.

Volta do Mar

I. LOSS CORRESPONDENCE

Where the wind shreds prayers, on a dark
sea road, things loosen, lose

their form. Unstring the ocean's grammar. Worry
the beads of its clauses. Let your fingertips

find each verb's pulse: wash, hull, drown. Trace
tenses: past and future's crush.

Sever the subject from its time
and place, like a plane from the sky.

Unthread notes from the stave to dissolve
song. Stitch by stitch, unknit words' knots.

Fracture each limb. Unbraid the plait of chord
and breath. Slide each phrase from the library

of connections. Words are sand, strand: grit
and brine, silent, beyond harrows.

2. WATER NEEDLES

Everyone is asleep but the sea, knotting, un-
knotting the rope of its own approach, squall-racked

nerve-running, steepening its crests. Night sea
shucks its quivering foil. Secrets spill

like shells, like waves under moongold brightwork.
The ocean's skeleton factory draws its hush

and din over the seabed. A sunken cutter
shifts and sighs. Fish thread its bones, dart, needles

between seams. Hands of the dead cast off
on silence. Night's bright teeth bite down on shore's

lip: cold foam, jangle of tangling weed,
wrack and trash, returning what remains

to this fluent shrine, angled memorial
to sea burial, to mute and godless prayer.

Hopeshred (t, s, h)

for Nathan Shepherdson

Three letters slip from a word. We lose
what falls out of alignment, unnameable:

every name a collection of letters
not sent, or returned to sender. Trans-

lated, written in the margins, held.
Three letters lodge in the spine. No-one

but you might remember them. Nameless
you walk over night's ache, treading

its blisters like grapes. Among sleepers
you witness lost letters, answers

knotted in anagrams. You believe nothing
cannot transpose itself, cannot trans-

duce. I imagine you, walking over
the border, leaving an old passport

vertical as *I* crossing to meet
new avenues, gain, a new name.

Grace

Whether to isles enchanted –
She bent her docile sails –

– Emily Dickinson

Blood Days: Monochords

1.

Dawn clouds, red as history, press down: I linger under sky-soft counterpane.

2.

Bells that peel the day into segments.

3.

Seams of lost memories: I speak to children about forgetting.

4.

Rising, a flush that says the muse is on her head: the weight of it, the deciding-to.

5.

The storm of adolescence again: umbrella behind me.

6.

Bloodcycles: at the lockers, red weather of circles cramped and guarded.

7.

The watch her father left no longer works, nor the floor they watch her from.

8.

My last school residency, three years ago: in a stroke of red your short life crossed out.

9.

Small voices bring me to my knees.

On Carrying: Seven Cledons

I.

In meetings academics say
I'll take carriage of this or, more likely
You can take carriage of this
In this way careers are built
block by block, in cells
from dreams of freedom

I made one myself
heat, grit, conviction
poetry, charge

When it hummed, ticked
ready to explode or implode
I left it, set it down
like a package at a train station

a bundle on hospital steps

2.

When you'd gone, a book slid from its lodge
Auden's *Letters from Iceland*
Practising bibliomancy
or distraction, I read

of hearts' desires
– their bend and whorl
Better never, says Auden
to be born

In *Away From Her* a retired academic
reads this to his vanishing wife
She replies: all they might
aspire to now
is *a little bit of grace*

Grace, with its small heart beating

3.

Balancing Plath's Second
Woman, knotted in argument
with generation itself

(Is it so difficult
for the spirit to conceive
a face
a mouth?)

with Leonard Cohen, who
sets his father's death
apart, beyond judgement
and dispute. I felt dispute
loosen itself from within when you

abjured your body, and mine

4.

Here's a question
for the gods, the forum, for
the empty room and its angels:
If I had chosen to fail
completely at one thing
what should it have been?

Not creativity: glorious making
obliquely displayed
in your every step and cell

When our chalk bones crumble
'Where Do We Go But Nowhere?'

Did I run too fast, generate too much
heat? Forget you for a moment?

Try again is *shut up* in a cold tongue

5.

I'd planted basil, rosemary, a lemon tree
Carried pots, soil, watering can:
queen of composition, poet of fronds
and hope. That winter: foliage going back
to earth. Underground, dividing
and multiplying, occult under mulch
each cell grew daily more specific

Neither hard wish nor soft
prayer puts leaves back
on branches. Every petal
goes to ground. Around me that spring
leaf-waving trees, not mine
Underfoot, compost

smiles for other peoples' babies

6.

An email offering a teddy bear remote
child locator capable of saying
when pressed
Mummy, I'm here

Your father, waiting for a friend
plays a poker machine
wins copiously: *your lucky day, mate!*

A colleague's Flaubertian email
signature: every particle
of life carries
poetry within it

At home, still
no-one speaks a word to me

Poetry, particles settle

7.

Weeks later on a train
to deliver a paper, I find
booties, jammed pink in the seat

beside me. Someone calls
as I get off the train
you left something!

The world is making and losing
putting things down, leaving them
wanting, listening for angels
professing one thing or another

For all the whispered wisdom
of wish and want, you either

carry something or you don't

Strand

Every poem has a secret addressee. Every secret
a shoreline. Mine loosens
like a tooth.

I wake to three knocks. Three times no-one
there. Knocks echo through an empty house until
I am empty of dreams.

An owl at noon means death. Your death
eyeing me, still, from a tree
one leafless noon.

See yourself in a dream: you are soon
to die. Seeing you, without me, in a dream, I knew
you could survive.

Tumble of wings into pane. A wrecked bird
huddled on the ledge, looking in. Your eyes
closed against pain.

Nothing to say, as when words lose their letters
in winter. Letters' spines dismantle
in my silent hand.

I hear your name in a dream of sea. Dream
my secrets fall from my mouth, braced
neat as pearls.

Broken mirror, spilt salt, opened
umbrella. Salt rain broke and I thought no
harm could come to you.

Never rock an empty chair. Your empty
room, fulcrum of consolation
and despair.

A sailor with an earring cannot drown. Drownless
in the hold of your sea cradle,
distant as shoreline.

Three

Three things in human life are important. The first is to be kind. The second is to be kind. And the third is to be kind.

– Henry James

It is you who smooths the quilt over
my sleep-shards, you
who do not yet live here,
but blaze silently.

•

My hand in this injury, if not
in its stitching.
Where do I look, if not
always to escape?

•

Compassion's small font: words folded back
or care-drafted.
Needlekind, brine, witness
to both wound and cure.

•

Patiently, sitting on hospice bed-
edge, you adjust
the leaky cannula
tune its little reed.

•

Holding – not your all, yet, though you rest
your head against
mine – space. Be patient. Trust
stirring in the bud.

•

Triage dreams: sirens, emergencies
ordered, borders
unsealed. Always alone
when pain climbs to ten.

•

The one who lost the most gives away
more. A giving
like soap to blade, salvaged
hope, ocean-rope, gauze.

•

When you are in danger, who am I
with such small gifts:
a poultice of godless
prayer, mute infusion.

•

Obscure calculus: abacus beads
falling like teeth.
And from your own torn mouth:
consolation, calm.

•

You know how to hold space: strange physics
with me, without
need, demand: where mourning
ebbs, lives next to love.

•

All threads in a weave of kin, all roots
that take you down
to glasswords sandbroken
ground small beyond sound.

•

Where all tongues lose their language, all hands
let go, forget
force, put down their cudgels –

Where all that divides
us calculates its losses and I
am made to learn

grace, in the place silence
breaks, bruises open
dark sails – I want to know one thing, try

to hold it, try
again, to be kind, to
be kind, kind.

Heartland

By what mystic mooring –
She is held today –

– Emily Dickinson

Were my whole insides a piece of sea, was I nothing but salty water with a mind of its own, was I some kind of fountain, was I the force of water through stone?

– Ali Smith

Interval

Your absence weighs more
than the stretch
                    of your body
over mine: sinewy, pinioning

hard as the moon that asks the moon-
flower to raise its face,
                              unfold
its petals to the dark. Then sets.

Sunturn

I waited for you winterlong
– Neil Young

Midwinter. Black
sun in motion, even
at its still point. Long

the winter, long
this night, this
waiting. In its white

moment no
momentum, still
the flicker of our name. Keep

me in the light
love, while you
winter alone. The tide

pulls back to come
forwards, holds itself
into itself. Now

things pull, tip
from stasis, lean
into new. Slow

fold of year
into year, past
into fiction. Break

the stride
of dark spirits, outpace
their company. Step

with me gold where others
walked, ghosted
by future suns.

Waiting Room

I.

Your absence lays its shadow on my skin.
A shadow's weight is measured by the dark.
Moonflowers open velvet to the night.
You brought the wrong brand of abandon, love.

A shadow's weight is measured by the dark
moon's tongue shivering on my thigh.
You brought the wrong brand of abandon. Love,
your craft's ahead, mine follows in its wake.

The moon's tongue flickers on my thigh.
You light a row of candles, soft as hymns
you craft. I follow in their wake.
Songless hull, ghost footsteps creak. Above,

you light a row of candles. Soft as hymns
or moonflowers' velvet in the night.
Songless hull. Ghost footsteps creak above
your absence, their shadow on my skin.

2.

No room for a shadow between us.
Nothing weighs more than your song's lift.
Moonflowers fold their secrets into light.
A time to be slow. A time for abandon:

nothing weighs more. Our song's lift
forgets the moon. The tidal pull's our
time to be slow, our time for abandon.
Blaze of harmonica, smoulder of your voice.

Forget the moon, the tidal pull's yours.
Two boats bump the shore, the shallows pulse
to the blaze of harmonica, shouldering my voice:
Music floods the hull. Our ghosts set sail.

Two boats bump the shore, the shallows pulse.
Moonflowers fold our secrets into light.
Music floods the hull. Our ghosts set sail.
Never again a shadow between us.

Carpus Diem

(wrist mnemonics)

Scaphoid, lunate, triquetrum – while I burn
to learn your body, we have time – we take
our time, it's a given – so let me focus, let me
be methodical as a med student late
at night – cram details of you into my skin's
memory – then linger like sacrament,
relish, fetish. Why think

about your wrists? Once so heavy
with shyness I couldn't lift my eyes – could
barely speak, watched your hands – proximal, distal
crease, distal row – thinking: to hold it all – to hold
this? It was charged. Marvellous. We were
early. Our arms were full like hearts in
poems – full of patience, pause – is there something

wrong with me? You'd know. I wake at night – dream
your DSM spills lines of poems. Let hands
do what lips do: learn, learn, trace the way
your smile curves or your— have I said how
glad I am, you are? Remember, photos
of pisiform (in gardening glove), trapezium
(stirring gravy), trapezoid (holding swimming

goggles) – don't forget capitate, hamate – don't
forget a hair, a pore, a breath of what is here
as it is: Sam Likes To Push The Toy Car Hard
and Some Lovers Try Positions That They
Can't Handle. Remember, we are spirits
caught in fretwork – matrix of hope and bone –
strong, flexible, holding, pushing, trying.

Bridge Physics

Two major forces act on a bridge at any given time: compression and tension. Compression, or compressive force, is a force that acts to compress or shorten the thing it is acting on. Tension, or tensile force, is a force that acts to expand or lengthen the thing it is acting on.

– teachengineering.org

And you there, here, near as the song
of what is silent: current
pulse and prayer of unbroken
deals, real: kin, fuel
heart and hearth of it, compressed: bridge
held strong, all along. Steady
on, you said. Steady, on: your voice
breath, grit, (wrists), you do me
good.   Tension, breakage, world's gone
wrong, but song, trust, bone, truth, keep
on unbroken: brakes on, bridge held, right
by me. Right by you. Strong
like someone singing, long, across
decades: precious, steady, strong-

hold on silence. Steady pulse, its decades-
long bridge across our separate singing, like
you by me: right. Strong, like night-rites
breaking open, holding our secrets, brakes
off, singing. Bone of truth and trust, wrong-
ful injuries wring their tension out.   The good
you do me, I do you. Your (wrists), grit, breath
voice – steady on. Steady. On. You said
all along you'd hold strong. Bridge
compressing past and future: the ravine of now, heart
and hearth: kin, fuel, the real
deal of prayer unbroken by words. Pulse
and current. The silence of what is:
you, here, near as this song.

Thirteen Uses for a Poem

1.

Subversion plank,
skulduggery spade,
drear-rake: late-
night infomercial all-
muck-cleaning marvel.

2.

Slice prized stanzas: line
cake tins. Bite into
splinters. Imprints:
Let me count. Let me.
Count me. Ways.

3.

Lotus cracking water's
lens. Hot-lit fish slip
by *within fierce*
flames: blue shadows
glide, lucid.

4.

Dive or catch: swung
floorward, flung
askew, loaf in thrum
& pummel: let yourself be
sand-kneaded, foam-leavened.

5.

Dispel bell, for desk
bedside or pocket. Clang
after a gutful
of harp & carp
cruel & fool.

6.

Unbend in its quiet. Soles
impressed with sea-
bed grains, you
arrow to hope: aching
airwards.

7.

A screen. Behind, slip
into nakedness. Project
jagged fragments, ouija-
wish, summon
& lantern your hidden.

8.

Fill with potting mix. Press
seeds deep: blossom-
watch, tear, shake
spin, chew, spit
green phonemes.

9.

Library of lost things, except
yours. Instead,
forgotten jetsam:
scraps of unlabelled
prayers whispering silence.

10.

Fold to hold jamb &
sash open for grace to cough
on coals, oddity to shiver
fingertips through every
secret's fold.

11.

Reminder: e.g. *Live ardently*
Remind me on a day: all, alarm, repeat
Remind me at a location: current location
Priority: !!!
Notes (archaic, lit.): burning, glowing.

12.

Like dreamtrace, flakes
of memory or love's
foreshadow, let it
stay with you, kick
its slippers under your bed.

13.

Prescription, perhaps illegible
scrawled by your doctor
of gall & glia, conductor
of cells' tenor, tonic
for idiopathic woes.

Inclined

after Bob Dylan's 'Make You Feel My Love'

The word love *is merely a sign that means something*
like the way to the mountain.

– Mark Doty

What the mountain thinks, you can't
know. When it leans the weight of its shadow
on you, tall, how much might it say in fall
or thrall, like a lover, telling all? You don't
know, but something's in step, like (black and blue)
and (avenue), and you, all backpack and crampon, ice-
axe your way through, poster girl for grit: you can't
wait, think of love as losing wait, court
waitlessness, ascend, impatient as snow, don't know
how, don't know where melt becomes avalanche, figure
stunts and chutzpah are the go, don't
know what you can't know, find yourself
lost, but (stars appear), so step by step, go
up, (dry your tears), keep in mind the rhyme

(rain on face) (warm embrace) the rhyme
of it, the pulse, climbing in iambics, and you can
know, you stumble, skirt the glacier, syncopate, or trip
and have to use your little kit, your grit, you do
know, though it's nothing you've known, find
you've left behind flat foothills, the boot in the ice
face, powder and slide. And you climb, patient: find you can
wait, watch the mountain waking to remember (rolling sea)
speechful, whistling love whispers (wild and free)
and the summit isn't some mystery since you do

know its song, its height and gaze, its quietude
and seep of calm, the way this climb takes heart
and breath from you, and gives them back, lighter,
can never be known, but walking here, you do know.

Notes

The title *A Kinder Sea* is inspired by Michael Burch's translation of a poem attributed to Plato: 'Mariner, do not ask whose tomb this may be, but go with good fortune; I wish you a kinder sea.' Used with the kind permission of Michael Burch. 'I wish you a kinder sea' is widely imagined to be from a letter by Emily Dickinson; however, this appears to be a myth. Thank you to Ross Gibson for help in ascertaining this.

'Sound Bridge' collects fragments from Mozart's 'Lacrimosa', Rilke's *The Duino Elegies* and Bob Dylan's 'You Angel, You'. The line 'Who, if I cried out, would hear me?' is from *The Poetry of Rainer Maria Rilke* by A. S. Kline (translation copyright © 2009), and is reproduced with the kind permission of Mr Adam David Kline.

'A Corner of the Sea' contains an epigraph by Emily Dickinson: 'Whether my bark went down at sea –'. This text is available under the Creative Commons Attribution – Share Alike License.

'Glass Letters' contains an epigraph by Paul Celan, translated by John Felstiner, from *Paul Celan: Poet, Survivor, Jew*: 'A poem [...] can be a message in a bottle, sent out in the – not always greatly hopeful – belief that somewhere and sometime it could wash up on land, on heartland perhaps.' Reproduced with the kind permission of Yale Representation Limited through PLSclear.

'Carmine Horizon' contains an epigraph by Mireille Juchau from *The World Without Us*: 'the clouds are shredded along a carmine horizon'. Reproduced with the kind permission of Mireille Juchau and Bloomsbury Publishing.

'Yellow' contains an epigraph from William Carlos Williams's 'Love Song', available in *Al Que Quiere!: A Book of Poems* (The Four Seas Company, 1917).

'Confetti by Dada' contains an epigraph by Tristan Tzara from *Dada Manifesto on Feeble Love and Bitter Love*: 'a lie that I have FIXED like a butterfly on a hat' and the line 'I still consider myself very likeable'. Reproduced with the kind permission of Molotov Editions.

'In Search of the Miraculous' contains an epigraph by Emily Dickinson: 'Whether she met with gales –'. This text is available under the Creative Commons Attribution – Share Alike License.

'Equal Footing Mermaids' quotes a telegram from Donald Crowhurst, which appears in *The Strange Last Voyage of Donald Crowhurst* by Nicholas Tomalin and Ron Hall:

> STRICKEN GOUT FOLLOWING
> NEWYEAR SHERRY PARTY
> NOW EQUAL FOOTING MERMAIDS STOP
> ALMOST INTO FORTIES

Reproduced with the kind permission of McGraw-Hill Education.

'Underwater Caulking' draws on the experiences of Robin Knox-Johnston, the first person to perform a single-handed non-stop circumnavigation of the globe. It quotes from his book *A World of My Own*: 'I still worried about the floors, but no more than I worried about the keel bolts or hull fastenings.' Reproduced with the kind permission of Robin Knox-Johnston.

'Disappearing Act' refers to artworks by Dutch-born conceptual artist Bas Jan Ader, including 'I'm too sad to tell you' (1970–71) and 'thoughts unsaid, then forgotten' (1973). Bas Jan Ader disappeared at sea during a solo voyage that was part of an artwork titled 'In Search of the Miraculous'.

'Volta do mar' or 'volta do mar logo' is a Portuguese phrase meaning 'turn of the sea' or 'return from the sea'. It refers to a navigational technique discovered in the fifteenth century.

'Hopeshred (t, s, h)' refers to Paul Celan's name change from Antschel to the anagrammatic Celan, dropping the letters t, s and h.

'Grace' contains an epigraph by Emily Dickinson:

> Whether to isles enchanted –
> She bent her docile sails –

This text is available under the Creative Commons Attribution – Share Alike License.

'On Carrying: Seven Cledons': Cledonism or cledonomancy is a form of divination dating back to classical antiquity. It involves chance findings of words overheard or stumbled upon, thought to carry messages. The suite includes a quotation from Sylvia Plath's *Three Women*: 'Is it so difficult

/ For the spirit to conceive a face, a mouth?' Reproduced with the kind permission of Faber and Faber Ltd. It also includes allusions to W. H. Auden's *Letter's from Iceland*, Lian Lunson's documentary *Leonard Cohen: I'm Your Man*, 'The Boatman's Call' (Mute Records) by Nick Cave and the Bad Seeds, and Gustave Flaubert's *Madame Bovary*.

'Three' contains an epigraph from Henry James in Leon Edel's *Henry James: A Life Vol. V, The Master*: 'Three things in human life are important. The first is to be kind. The second is to be kind. And the third is to be kind.'

'Heartland' contains two epigraphs:

- Emily Dickinson's:

  By what mystic mooring –
  She is held today –

  This text is available under the Creative Commons Attribution – Share Alike License.
- Ali Smith's from *Girl Meets Boy: The Myth of Iphis*: 'Were my whole insides a piece of sea, was I nothing but salty water with a mind of its own, was I some kind of fountain, was I the force of water through stone?'

'Sunturn' contains an epigraph from Neil Young's 'Winterlong': 'I waited for you winterlong'.

'Carpus Diem' includes mnemonics used by medical students to learn the names of the bones in the hand.

'Bridge Physics' contains an epigraph from *Hands-on Activity: Bridge Types: Tensile & Compressive Forces, Regents of the University of Colorado*: 'Two major forces act on a bridge at any given time: compression and tension. Compression, or compressive force, is a force that acts to compress or shorten the thing it is acting on. Tension, or tensile force, is a force that acts to expand or lengthen the thing it is acting on.'

'Thirteen Uses for a Poem' includes slivers of two other poems: Elizabeth Barrett Browning's 'Sonnet 43' ('How do I love thee?') and 'Monkey' by Wu Cheng'en ('even amidst fierce flames the golden lotus can be planted') in the translation on Sylvia Plath's gravestone.

'Inclined' contains an epigraph from Mark Doty's *Dog Years: A Memoir*: 'The word love is merely a sign that means something like the way to the mountain'. It also borrows rhymes from Bob Dylan's 'Make You Feel My Love'.

Acknowledgements

Most of this work was written on the land of the Eora nation. I acknowledge the traditional custodians and pay my respects to Elders past, present and emerging.

Grateful acknowledgement is made to the editors of the following journals and anthologies for publishing versions of these poems: *The Best Australian Poems 2011*, *2012* (ed. John Tranter), *2013* (ed. Lisa Gorton), *2014* (ed. Geoff Page), *Rabbit Poetry Journal*, *Australian Book Review*, *Cordite Poetry Review*, *Arc* (Canada), Montreal International Poetry Prize *Global Poetry Anthology 2015*, Montreal International Poetry Prize *Global Poetry Anthology 2017*, *The Turnrow Anthology of Contemporary Australian Poetry* (ed. John Kinsella), *Contemporary Australian Feminist Poetry: The Hunter Anthology* (eds Bonny Cassidy and Jessica L. Wilkinson), *Prayers of a Secular World* (eds Jordie Albiston and Kevin Brophy), *Axon*, *The Australian*, *Once Wild: Newcastle Poetry Prize Anthology 2014*, *Connective Tissue: Newcastle Poetry Prize Anthology 2015*, *the crows in town: Newcastle Poetry Prize Anthology 2017*, *<O>PEN* (ed. Pascalle Burton), *Tincture Journal*, *Stylus*, *Empathy: Poems from the 2018 ACU Prize for Poetry* and *Signs: The University of Canberra Vice-Chancellor's International Poetry Prize 2018* (eds Jen Webb and Donna Maree Hanson).

'Sound Bridge' was awarded second place in the 2018 Australian Catholic University Prize for Poetry. An earlier version of 'Becoming the Sea' won the 2014 Nillumbik Ekphrasis Poetry Award. 'Anomiidae' was commissioned by Red Room Company.

This book was supported by a grant from the Australia Council, for which I am deeply grateful.

I am exceptionally fortunate in the people who have worked with me to prepare this book for publication. To have had a poet and critic of Lisa Gorton's calibre as my editor has been a joy and privilege. Thank you to my publisher, Aviva Tuffield, for her energy, vision and enthusiasm, and to everyone at UQP, especially Felicity Dunning for her professionalism, calm and care, and Sandy Cull for her ever-magnificent cover design.

Thank you to Stuart Barnes and Judith Bishop who read earlier versions of this manuscript. Your generosity, talent and kindness have shaped these poems.

Thank you to the wonderful friends who have discussed some of these poems with me, especially Bernard Cohen, Ali Alizadeh, Mireille Juchau, Justin Clemens, Amanda O'Callaghan, Simon Tedeschi and Anna Jacobson.

Thanks, too, to Anna for her indefatigable and gracious support with the permissions-seeking process.

To the man who retyped the poem I lost, among many other supportive, inspiring and gravity-defying acts, thank you.

Thank you, Benjamin and Imogen. *A Kinder Sea* has been made as you have grown up. You are everywhere here, and everything to me.

Other UQP poetry titles

VANISHING POINT
Felicity Plunkett

Winner of the 2008 Thomas Shapcott Poetry Prize
Shortlisted for the WA Premier's Book Awards (Poetry)
Shortlisted for the ACT Judith Wright Poetry Prize
Shortlisted for the Anne Elder Award

The moon's face removes itself
behind cloud's purdah,
the way you must move, ethical,
with what has lodged,
and what is to come,
fabricated into glitter.

Opening with a surreal vision of creativity and mourning, *Vanishing Point* returns to flakes of desire, memory and dreams. This dynamic collection traces currents of eroticism and the imagination, charting the skeleton of feeling and the blood of beginnings.

> '*Vanishing Point* is a remarkable achievement. Plunkett's range, poise and passion are striking. This is a collection which shows a high order of poetry.' Julian Croft

> '*Vanishing Point* counterbalances lyrical grace with a wild formalism. Plunkett knows that amazement is hard-won, and her voice is a guide through light and dark, chaos and order.' Anthony Lawrence

ISBN 978 0 7022 3721 8

UQP

INTERVAL
Judith Bishop

Winner of the 2019 NSW Premier's Literary Awards – Kenneth Slessor Prize for Poetry

Come near, let me
sense you, in this human
way we have – for now
and not forever.

Judith Bishop's attentive gaze unfailingly reveals the luminous. In *Interval*, her poems – many addressed to a lover or to children – explore intimacy, solitude and the 'chemical mess' of human love.

> 'These poems are vibrant, clear and sparse: each line sends a numinous pulse deep into the book. Bishop's clean-cut lines begin their slow burn and you know you are in the hands of a consummate technician.' Robert Adamson

> 'In the beauty of birth is the muteness of our existence on a planet we're destroying, and this paradox drives the book in a committed and deeply intelligent way.' John Kinsella

> '*Interval* is a supple exploration of consciousness and the mysterious space-time matrix from which change and growth arise. Judith Bishop takes us on a philosophical, singing search guided by human love.' Jan Owen

ISBN 978 0 7022 6007 0

UQP